BUILDING RELATIONSHIPS

PARENTS AND GUARDIANS

BY STEPHANIE FINNE

BLUE OWL
BOOKS

TIPS FOR CAREGIVERS

Social and emotional learning (SEL) helps children manage emotions, create and achieve goals, maintain relationships, learn how to feel empathy, and make good decisions. The SEL approach will help children establish positive habits in communication, cooperation, and decision-making. By incorporating SEL in early reading, children will be better equipped to build confidence and foster positive peer networks.

BEFORE READING

Talk to the reader about who parents and guardians are.

Discuss: What does a parent or guardian do? Who are your caregivers?

AFTER READING

Talk to the reader about building positive relationships with parents and guardians.

Discuss: What are some ways to build positive relationships with your parents or guardians? What can you do to show respect and communicate with them?

SEL GOAL

Communication is a big part of building strong relationships. One way to teach this skill is to model it. Being open and honest when talking to readers will show them how communication works. Discuss how learning communication skills can help them connect with others.

TABLE OF CONTENTS

CHAPTER 1

WE ARE FAMILY

Not all families look the same. You might have two dads or two moms. Your friend might have grandparents as **guardians**. Parents and guardians are caregivers. They care for, teach, and love us.

Sometimes caregivers and children aren't related **biologically**. Some families don't live together all the time. No matter what a family looks like, **relationships** with caregivers are important. Building healthy relationships with them helps us learn to get along with other people in our lives.

Layla and Hazel's dad coaches their soccer team. Their mom is at every game to cheer them on. Layla and Hazel thank their parents for their **support**. This support and **appreciation** brings the family closer together.

SHOW SUPPORT

Supporting another person means you are there for them, even during hard times. You cheer them on.

Olivia's parents are not married. Her dad lives in a different state. He shows his love by calling Olivia often. She shares her thoughts and feelings with him. By talking and being honest with each other, they continue building their relationship. Olivia knows she can **rely** on her dad, even if he is far away.

CHAPTER 2

WORKING TOGETHER

Part of being a family is working together. **Communicating** helps you and your caregivers work together. Talking about problems can help you find solutions.

Emmy lives with her grandparents. Sometimes she misses her mom and dad. She gets angry and acts out. Grandma calls a family meeting. Everyone talks about their feelings. After, they understand each other better. They make a plan to share stories about Emmy's parents more often.

Mason doesn't want to do chores. His dad talks to him. Their family is a team. Everyone needs to do their part. Mason understands now. He does chores without arguing. Mason's dad knows he can rely on him. Mason learns to be respectful and to ask questions when he doesn't understand or disagrees.

THE FAMILY TEAM

Every family is a team. You work together to make it strong. This means following family rules, supporting one another, and accepting each other's differences.

Julian's mom remarried. Julian was sad at first. For a long time, he wouldn't do what his stepfather, David, asked. His mom explains that David is there for both of them. Julian starts spending more time with David. They get along better. Now, Julian is happy he has another person who loves him!

CHAPTER 3

GETTING ALONG

You may not get along with your caregivers all the time. You may have disagreements. Sometimes you argue. But that doesn't mean you don't love each other.

Danny had a fight with his **foster parents**. He worries they will send him away. His foster father thanks him for sharing his feelings. He **reassures** him that won't happen. He loves and supports him. Danny **trusts** him more. Talking about his worries helps them build a stronger relationship.

John was **adopted** as a baby. Sometimes he feels like he doesn't fit in with his siblings. He gets sad. His parents respect his feelings. They are available when he wants to talk. John shares his feelings when he is ready. His parents listen. Their actions show him every day that they love him and his siblings the same.

ASK FOR HELP

Sometimes adults have a hard time controlling their emotions or actions. This is never your fault. Talk to another adult you trust if this happens often. They can get help for your family.

A healthy family shows support, kindness, and love to one another. Be kind, be supportive, and say "thank you" for the things your caregivers do for you. Parents and guardians love you. They help you grow.

GOALS AND TOOLS

GROW WITH GOALS

How can you build relationships with caregivers? Try these goals:

Goal: Make a list of things you can talk about with your caregivers. It can be a good part of your day. Maybe there is a grade you are proud of. You can tell a funny joke. Share this list with your caregivers. Talking helps you grow closer.

Goal: Spend time doing things you both enjoy. Go for a walk, play a game, cook together, or watch a show you like. Have fun together. This will help you feel closer.

Goal: It feels good to be appreciated. Show your caregivers love. Tell them you appreciate all they do. You can write a note, make a card, or draw a picture. Show you care about them.

WRITING REFLECTION

Think about a special time with your caregiver that made you feel good. What made you feel good? What did you do together or say to one another? Reflect on how their words and actions made you feel. Write about your emotions. What made you feel that way? Share what you wrote with your caregiver.

GLOSSARY

adopted
To be legally made the child of someone who is not a biological parent.

appreciation
A feeling of gratitude or admiration.

biologically
Related by genetics.

communicating
Sharing information, ideas, or feelings with another person through language, eye contact, or gestures.

foster parents
Temporary guardians of a child who has lost their parents or been removed from a parent's care.

guardians
People who legally care for children who are not their own.

reassures
Makes someone feel calm and confident.

relationships
Connections between two or more people.

rely
To depend on.

support
To give help, comfort, or encouragement.

trusts
Believes someone is honest and reliable.

TO LEARN MORE

FACT SURFER

Finding more information is as easy as 1, 2, 3.

1. Go to www.factsurfer.com
2. Enter "**parentsandguardians**" into the search box.
3. Choose your book to see a list of websites.

INDEX

Blue Owl Books are published by Jump!, 5357 Penn Avenue South, Minneapolis, MN 55419, www.jumplibrary.com

Copyright © 2025 Jump! International copyright reserved in all countries. No part of this book may be reproduced in any form without written permission from the publisher.

Library of Congress Cataloging-in-Publication Data

Names: Finne, Stephanie, author.
Title: Parents and guardians / by Stephanie Finne.
Description: Minneapolis, MN: Jump!, Inc., [2025]
Series: Building relationships | Includes index.
Audience: Ages 7–10
Identifiers: LCCN 2023054712 (print)
LCCN 2023054713 (ebook)
ISBN 9798892130059 (hardcover)
ISBN 9798892130066 (paperback)
ISBN 9798892130073 (ebook)
Subjects: LCSH: Parents–Juvenile literature. | Guardian and ward–Juvenile literature. | Families–Juvenile literature. | Interpersonal relations–Juvenile literature.
Classification: LCC HQ755.8 .F566 2025 (print)
LCC HQ755.8 (ebook)
DDC 306.874–dcundefined
LC record available at https://lccn.loc.gov/2023054712
LC ebook record available at https://lccn.loc.gov/2023054713

Editor: Katie Chanez
Designer: Emma Almgren-Bersie
Content Consultant: Lisa Meyers, PhD, LCSW

Photo Credits: fizkes/Shutterstock, cover, 11; Prostock-studio/Shutterstock, 1, 8–9; Dimple Bhati/iStock, 3; Drs Producoes/iStock, 4; JohnnyGreig/iStock, 5; Eric Raptosh Photography/Getty, 6–7; Wavebreakmedia/iStock, 10; kate_sept2004/iStock, 12–13; SeventyFour/Shutterstock, 14–15; NaMong Productions92/Shutterstock, 16; Milko/iStock, 17; AnnaStills/iStock, 18–19; IndianFaces/Shutterstock, 20–21.

Printed in the United States of America at Corporate Graphics in North Mankato, Minnesota.